CON

see it places

buy it places

watch it places to be entertained   **26**

taste it places to eat and drink   **38**

know it practical information   **48**

directory hotel listings and more   **56**

speak it and **index**   **62**

Map references are denoted in the text by ❶ Greater San Diego
❷ Downtown ❸ Mission Bay ❹ La Jolla ❺ Tijuana.

san diego places to see

Lively, engaging San Diego sprawls around one of the finest natural bays in the world. Top of the list of its many attractions has to be the incredible weather, which makes it the perfect destination for sports-lovers and families. But the year-round sunshine is not all that San Diego has to offer: the myriad museums of Balboa Park display some of the finest art in California, and you can hop across the border to Tijuana in Mexico for a taste of a whole different culture. Add to that glorious beaches and dramatic cliffs and world-famous attractions like the San Diego Zoo and SeaWorld, and it's not hard to see why San Diego likes to call itself 'America's Finest City'.

see it places to see

Balboa Park

Balboa Park (❶) is a vast, lush expanse right in the heart of San Diego. It's crammed with museums and gardens, and shaded by hundreds of trees planted by the 19th-century botanist Kate Olivia Sessions. Many of the museums are set in beautiful, frothy pavilions built for two International Expositions held in 1915-16 and in 1935-36, and the Visitor Center, which should be your first stop for maps and information, is housed in a sumptuous Spanish Colonial-style mansion.

Close to the Visitor Center are two of the park's finest museums: the San Diego Museum of Art, with works from Renaissance painting to challenging contemporary art; and the delightful Timken Museum of Art, with a collection of European Old Masters, Russian icons, and fine American painting. Fans of planes, trains, and automobiles love the Aerospace Museum, Automotive Museum, and the Railroad Museum, and children delight in the high-tech, interactive Reuben H Fleet Science Center, which has everything from space-flight simulators to planetarium shows. If it all gets too much, linger in the peaceful Japanese Friendship Garden.

This is just a selection of highlights – the park contains 15 museums; find details of all of them from the Park Information Center. Look out for the enormous Spreckel's Organ in its own pavilion; there are free concerts each Sunday at 2pm. A free trolley service operates in the park, and tram stops are marked on the park map.

Façade of the Aerospace Museum

Aerospace Museum ❶ 6D
Adm. Open 10am-4.30pm, until 5.30pm in summer. T: 619 234 8291, www.aerospacemuseum.org

Balboa Park Passes
The Park Information Center sells the Passport to Balboa Park for $30, which gives admission to 13 attractions within the park; for an extra $25, you can add Deluxe Admission to San Diego Zoo, on the edge of the park.

The Japanese Friendship Garden

Automotive Museum ❶ 5E
Adm. Open 10am-5pm daily. T: 619 231 2886, www.sdautomuseum.org

Japanese Friendship Garden ❶ 4F
Open 10am-4pm Tue-Sun.
T: 619 232 2721, www.niwa.org

Museum of Photographic Arts ❶ 4G
Adm. Open 10am-5pm daily, until 9pm Thu. T: 619 238 7559, www.mopa.org

Natural History Museum ❶ 4H
Adm. Open 10am-5pm daily, until 5.30pm in summer. T: 619 232 3821, www.sdnhm.org

Reuben H Fleet Science Center ❶ 4H
Adm. Open 9.30am-5pm Mon-Thu, 9.30am-9pm Fri-Sat, 9.30am-6pm Sun. T: 619 238 1233, www.rhfleet.org

San Diego Model Railroad Museum ❶ 4G
Adm. Open 11am-4pm Tue-Fri, 11am-5pm Sat-Sun. T: 619 696 0199, www.sdmodelrailroadm.com

Balboa Park for Free
Each museum has free admissions on one Tuesday per month:

First Tuesday
Reuben H Fleet Science Center, Railroad Museum, Natural History Museum.

Second Tuesday
Museum of Photographic Arts, Historical Society Museum.

Third Tuesday
Japanese Friendship Garden, Mingei International, SDAI Museum of the Living Artist, San Diego Museum of Art, Museum of Man.

Fourth Tuesday
Aerospace Museum, Automotive Museum, International Cottages, Hall of Champions, Hall of Nations Film.

San Diego Museum of Art ❶ 4F
Adm. Open 10am-6pm Tue-Sun, until 9pm Thu. T: 619 232 7931, www.sdmart.org

Timken Museum of Art ❶ 4G

*Open 10am-4.30pm Tue-Sat, 1.30pm-
4.30pm Sun. T: 619 239 5548,
www.timkenmuseum.org*

Sights & Hoods

Coronado ❷ 5A & ❶ 4B

The long thin spit which is Coronado
hooks up over the southern end of
the Bay of San Diego. The navy have
taken over half of it, and you can see
their enormous aircraft carriers and
ships from miles around. The rest of
Coronado remains a quiet, sleepy
community of clapboard shops and
houses more reminiscent of New
England than southern California.

Beach at Coronado with toll bridge behind

The Mission-style San Diego train station

It's connected to the mainland by
a dramatically curving bridge, or
you can take the ferry, which gives
fabulous views of the city at night.
You can't miss Coronado's most
famous sight, the huge, white Hotel
Del Coronado (affectionately known
as 'the Del', *see p.57*) which was
built in the 19th century and sits
overlooking the long sandy beach.
The Del has featured in dozens of
Hollywood films, most famously in
Some Like It Hot.

Downtown ❷ 4G

After years of neglect, San Diego's
downtown is now well and truly on
the up. It's one of the liveliest
neighborhoods for shopping and
nightlife, and glittering new high-rise
offices and hotels make for a
dramatic skyline, particularly at
night. The heart of downtown is the
Horton Plaza (*see p.24*), a colorful
outdoor shopping mall and
entertainment center. Along the
seafront, visit the original Maritime

Museum (❷ 2B), set in a series of historic boats including the lovely *Star of India*, the oldest active sailing ship in the world. Close by is the

The famous 'Del' in Coronado

Entrance to the Museum of Contemporary Art

Santa Fe train station, a charming mission-style building with two pretty tiled domes. Opposite it is the ultra-modern downtown branch of the Museum of Contemporary Art (❷ 3C), based in La Jolla (*see p.8*), which offers a varied program of contemporary art and all kinds of activities including film screenings and poetry readings. There are child-orientated events (*see p.59*) and more opportunities for souvenir shopping and entertainment at the Seaport Village on the waterfront.
Maritime Museum: Adm. Open 9am-8pm, until 9pm in summer. T: 619 234 9153, www.sdmaritime.com
Museum of Contemporary Art: *open 11am-5pm Thu-Tue. T: 619 234 1001, www.mcasd.org*

Gaslamp Quarter ❷ 5E

The historic Gaslamp Quarter covers 16 blocks in the heart of downtown San Diego. The Victorian-style buildings were constructed during the late 19th century, but the area soon slid into disrepute after flophouses and brothels sprang up

Restored façade in the Gaslamp Quarter

in the formerly grand mansions. A dramatic restoration project has returned many of the historic buildings to their former glory, and the area is now San Diego's most popular neighborhood for thriving bars and restaurants. You'll find information and a small museum of local history in the William Heath Davis House (*410 Island Ave, T: 619 233 4692,*

Trendy Hillcrest by night

Sleeping seals on the beach at La Jolla

www.gaslampquarter.org) which also runs walking tours of the district (*see p.55*). Many of the most striking buildings are located along Fifth Ave, including the Backesto Building (*No. 614*), the Mercantile Building (*No. 822*), and the whimsical Louis Bank of Commerce (another former brothel) with its twin towers (*No. 835*).

Museum of Contemporary Art in La Jolla

Hillcrest ❶ 3B

Hillcrest is one of San Diego's trendiest neighborhoods, and home to the city's relaxed gay community. This is a great area for finding fashionable bars, shops, and restaurants, and you can rummage at dozens of great vintage clothes stores and quirky bookstores.

La Jolla & Torrey Pines State Reserve ❶ 1A, ❹

The smart seaside suburb of La Jolla (pronounced 'La Hoya') is located about nine miles north of downtown San Diego. The elegant boutiques along Girard Ave and Prospect St reflect the chic residents' tastes, and La Jolla is also home to some of the city's finest restaurants. The rocky, cave-pocked coastline around La Jolla Cove – perhaps the most famous postcard shot in San Diego – has been declared an ecological reserve, and you'll find all kinds of marine life in the rock pools and beaches. You can reach the caves via a steep, slippery staircase in the Cave

Rugged cliffs and beach at Torrey Pines State Reserve

Shop (*1325 Cave St*), which also has an English tea room. The cliff-top Museum of Contemporary Art offers striking ocean views to go with its excellent collection of paintings, sculpture, and photography, and has a terraced sculpture garden at the back. Just behind the museum, a colony of seals have adopted a small cove as their home. There are more aquatic creatures a little farther up the coast at the fascinating Birch Aquarium at Scripps, with more than 30 tanks, and simulated submarine

rides and earthquakes. The rooftop tide pool offers breath-taking views of the coastline, and there are special whale-watching events during the winter. Just north of here is the spectacular Torrey Pines State Reserve, a beautiful cliff-top park filled with hiking trails and overlooking a glorious sandy beach. *Museum of Contemporary Art: 700 Prospect St, La Jolla. Adm. Open 11am-5pm Sun-Tue, Fri-Sat, 11am-7pm Thu. T: 858 454 3541, www.mcasd.org*

Birch Aquarium at Scripps: 2300 Expedition Way. Adm. Open 9am-5pm daily. T: 858 534 FISH, www.aquarium.ucsd.edu

Mission Beach & Pacific Beach
❶ 2A/❶

Mission Beach is probably the most popular beach in San Diego, an endless stretch of golden sand that is perfect for families. Just north, laid-back, breezy Pacific Beach is a lively surfing neighborhood on a slim strip of land dividing Mission Bay from the Pacific. There are plenty of bars, restaurants, shops, and funfairs, and

flocks of joggers, rollerbladers, and cyclists come to enjoy the boardwalk that backs both beaches.

Ocean Beach ❶ 3A

Ocean Beach is a small, mainly residential neighborhood about 5 miles (8 km) northwest of downtown San Diego. A typically relaxed Californian beach community, it has resolutely refused

to allow big chain shops and high-rise buildings to develop here. The main street, Newport Avenue, is lined with soaring palm trees and an engaging mixture of laid-back bars, hip boutiques, antique shops, and burger joints. Gaggles of young surfers pile up to the beach, and a spindly fishing pier juts out into the ocean. The northern tip of the peninsula is home to Dog Beach,

Stormy evening at Point Loma lighthouse

Things That Go Bump In the Night

The Whaley House (*Old Town* ❶ 2B) was built in 1856 for the entrepreneur Thomas Whaley, and is now a museum filled with period furnishings. But nobody comes to see the exhibits: they come to be spooked. The Whaleys have never left, and they, plus an assortment of pets, children, and other hangers on, have been haunting the property for decades.

where hundreds of dogs are allowed off the leash to run about and splash happily in the sea.

Old Town ❶ 2B

Old Town was the first European settlement in southern California and many of the oldest buildings have been preserved in the Old Town State Historic Park. Overlooking the main square is a replica of the 19th-century Robinson-Rose House, now a

Visitor Center (*San Diego Ave & Twiggs St*), which runs daily guided tours with costumed volunteers. Opposite is the elegant Casa de Estudillo (*San Diego Ave & Twiggs St*), a low, whitewashed adobe house set around gardens and filled with period furniture. Off the main square is the colorful Bazaar del Mundo, packed with souvenir shops and restaurants. Within the park, you'll find dentists, cigar shops, stables, general stores, and soap-makers selling traditional goods. Along San Diego Avenue is the El Campo Santo cemetery, burial place of gamblers, bandits, and aristocrats, and high on the Juan Street Hill is another collection of Victorian mansions that form the Old Town Heritage Park. Above these is Presidio Park, where the first mission in San Diego was established in the 18th century. The church and adjoining museum are open to visitors, and the lawns are favorite picnicking spots.

Point Loma ❶ 4A

In 1542, Juan Rodriguez Cabrillo (*see p.60*) claimed the bay of San Diego

The hippo at San Diego Zoo

for Spain. He stepped ashore at Point Loma, a narrow, cliff-edged peninsula that juts south across the bay, and a 144-acre area has been preserved as the Cabrillo National Monument. The Visitor Center has exhibits on his voyage, and information on the annual migration of the California gray whales (*see p.55*). There are two lighthouses: the oldest is a charming whitewashed building which has stood here since 1855 and can still be visited. The newer lighthouse, out on the very tip of the peninsula, was used as a

setting in *Top Gun*. There are tide pools under the western cliffs, which are also the best place to spot the whales in winter. *Cabrillo National Monument: Adm $5 per car. Open 9am-5.15pm daily. T: 619 557 5450, www.nps.gov/cabr*

San Diego Zoo & San Diego Wild Animal Park ❶

Spread out across canyons and hills on the northern fringe of Balboa Park (*see pp.4-5*), San Diego's zoo is the city's most famous attraction. Vast and hugely entertaining for children,

Bai Yun and baby Su Lin at the zoo

it's crammed with thousands of species, from polar bears to hippos, and there are all kinds of special events – including a fantastic sea lion show – which take place daily. Committed to conservation, the zoo is home to the only family of giant pandas in the US, and the California Condor Recovery Program has saved these beautiful birds from near extinction. Bus tours take the pain out of climbing up and down the steep canyons, and you can also sail across the park in the Skyfari Aerial Tram. Thirty-two miles (51 km) north of San Diego is the Zoo's sister park, the San Diego Wild Animal

Park, where more than 3,000 wild animals roam in their natural habitats. *San Diego Zoo: opens daily 9am, closing hours change seasonally. T: 619 234 3153 (times & prices), www.sandiegozoo.org.*
San Diego Wild Animal Park: opens daily 9am, closing hours change seasonally. T: 760 747 8702, www.wildanimalpark.org. Combined tickets to the Zoo, Wild Animal Park, & SeaWorld are available.

SeaWorld & Mission Bay ❶ 2A, ❸

Mission Bay is a 11,366-acre (4,600-ha) watery paradise for sports-lovers: sheltered beaches, picnic areas, hiking and cycling trails, and remarkably little commercial development have made it a hot spot for local families at weekends. The biggest attraction here is SeaWorld, one of the largest marine theme parks in the world. The daily shows – featuring dolphins, sea lions, otters, and, most famously,

Feed the bottlenose dolphins at SeaWorld

killer whales – are astounding, with incredible acrobatics and superb choreography. Other favorite attractions include the Penguin Encounter, and the Shark Encounter, which culminates with a tunnel through their enormous tank. At Rocky Point Preserve, feed – and pat – the bottlenose dolphins, or touch the slippery rays, and don't miss feeding time at the seal and sea lion pool. There are dozens of aquariums and fun rides. *SeaWorld: Adm. Open daily from 10am, closing hours vary seasonally. 500 Sea World Dr, Mission Bay, T: 619 226 3901, www.seaworld.com*

Tijuana ❺

Tijuana is a sprawling, chaotic, edgy frontier town just across the border in Mexico. Traditionally, it's been seen as a place for young Americans to party (avoiding the over-21 drinking law in the US) and a tax-free shopping zone. But there's more to Tijuana than meets the eye: walking down the most famous shopping street, Avenida Revolución (locally known as 'La Revo'), it's easy

to feel overwhelmed. But wander down any of the streets that splinter off La Revo, and you'll have a much more authentic experience of Mexican life. Find a small café for a spicy Mexican lunch of tacos or tamales – Super Antojitos (*1810 Calle 4a*) is good, and so is La Fonda de Don Pedro (*1623 Calle 2a*) – and then take a stroll with Mexican families in the manicured little Parque Teniente Guerrero. For a colorful array of pungent cheeses, neon-lit religious kitsch, herbs, and spices, head for the Pasaje Añagua (*off Calle 2a*), or take in the excellent Centro Cultural de Tijuana in the smart (but soulless) modern suburb of Zona Río.

Flipper plays to camera ...

Down Mexico Way

Don't drive if you can help it: there are queues at US border control on the return journey. The Blue Line trolley (*see p.51*) takes you to close to the border; stroll into Tijuana in 15 minutes or take a yellow taxi at the border. Citizens of the US, Canada, EU, Australia, and New Zealand do not need visas (you need a passport, or photo ID for US-citizens) to enter Mexico for less than 30 days. Check details with your Mexican embassy or consulate before making the trip.

Welcome to Tijuana

san diego places to shop

San Diego is a great place to shop. Locals like to shop at malls, vast complexes scattered across the city where you'll find the big department stores and all the major chains as well as restaurants and massive cinemas. The malls also offer convenience – and often amazing bargains – but it can be much more fun to browse among the boutiques of elegant La Jolla or trendy Hillcrest, or to check out the surfer shops in Pacific Beach. Recently San Diego has sprouted a series of quirky, individual shops selling everything from antiques to unusual fashion. Don't miss the daily farmers' markets for making up a picnic, and save your spending money for Tijuana, which is famously cheap and great for all kinds of unusual souvenirs.

buy it places to shop

Art & Antiques

Gallery Alexander ❹

Visit Gallery Alexander for original and stylish contemporary American furniture and crafts. Smaller pieces include charming ceramics, glassware, and jewelry – which make perfect gifts. The gallery also hosts several exhibitions a year, including the annual Teapot Show. *7925 Girard Ave, La Jolla, T: 858 459 9433.*

Many Hands ❷ 5E

There are over 30 members of this San Diego artists' co-operative based in the Gaslamp Quarter. They produce a variety of crafts, including jewelry, toys, woven baskets, and ceramics. *302 Island Ave, Suite 101, Gaslamp Quarter, T: 619 557 8303, www.manyhandscraftgallery.com*

Newport Ave Antique Center ❶ 3A

Newport Avenue, the main drag in Ocean Beach, is crammed with antique shops. Most of them are grouped together in a series of small, mall-style complexes like this one.

There's always a wide range of goods, from Japanese tea services to sturdy Victorian furniture, and from costume jewelry to old clothes. *4836 Newport Ave, Ocean Beach, T: 619 224 1994.*

Spanish Village Art Center ❶ 3G

Myriad tiny galleries and studios gathered together in a small complex in Balboa Park. See the artisans at work, and choose from all kinds of crafts – painted silks,

ceramics, painting, sculpture, and jewelry. *1770 Village Place, Balboa Park, T: 619 233 9050, www.spanishvillageart.com*

Unicorn Antiques Mall ❷ 5F

San Diego's largest antiques mall is set over three floors in an historic building. Prices reflect its popular location, but there is always a wide variety of antiques and collectibles. *704 J St, Gaslamp District, T: 619 232 1696.*

The entrance to Newport Ave Antique Center

Books & Music

Bluestocking Books ● 3B

A welcoming neighborhood bookstore in a charming district with an excellent selection of new, used, and out-of-print books, as well as a small collection of unusual prints, cards, and CDs. Mellow jazz is the perfect soundtrack for browsing, and there's a battered old sofa to sink into while you make your mind up. Also poetry readings. *3817 Fifth Ave, Hillcrest,*
T: 619 296 1424,
www.bluestockingbooks.com

M-Theory Music ● 5B

At M-Theory, the knowledgeable staff will introduce you to new bands or help you locate a hard-to-find favorite. As well as all the mainstream performers in most genres, it stocks a great range of local music by San Diego bands, hosts regular in-store performances, and turns itself into an art gallery on the last Thursday of each month. It also buys and sells used vinyl, CDs and DVDs. *3004 Juniper St, South Park, T: 619 269 2963,*
www.mtheorymusic.com

Warwick's Books ●

This elegant bookstore is an institution in La Jolla. It has been going for more than a century, and has a particularly good section on

Comforting surrounds at Bluestocking Books

Museum Stores

San Diego's museum stores offer a range of gifts. Go to the San Diego Zoo (*see p.11*) store for toys and crafts, to the Reuben H Fleet Science Center (*see p.5*) for electronic gizmos, the Museum of Art (*see p.5*) for posters, and the Museum of Contemporary Art (*see p.8*) for household goods.

San Diego. It also hosts regular readings. *7812 Girard Ave, La Jolla, T: 858 454 0347, www.warwicks.com*

Fashion

Gentleman's Quarter ❹
One of a string of upmarket boutiques in the exclusive La Jolla

Funky frontage at Raw

Elegant designs at Maddie Moon

Streetwise fashions in Mint, a streetwise store

neighborhood, this one is dedicated to elegant menswear, particularly specializing in European designers. *1200 Prospect St, La Jolla, T: 858 459 3351.*

Maddie Moon Designs ❸
Funky, colorful designs from this young San Diego designer: bright, affordable, and eye-catching hipster flares, skirts, and a great selection of amazing beaded disco dresses. *3725 Mission Blvd, Mission Beach, T: 858 488 9663.*

Mint ❶ 3B
This ultra-hip tunnel-like store in trendy Hillcrest is crammed with a floor-to-ceiling display of designer shoes at surprisingly reasonable prices. Besides streetwear classics from Adidas and Converse, you'll find sexy stilettos, boots, and adorable silk pumps. *525 University Ave, Hillcrest, T: 619 291 6468.*

Plasticland ❶ 3B
Whether you're going clubbing or just want to stand out from the

crowd, this boutique specializes in selling fashion-forward and edgy clothes for women, teens, and pre-teens. Everything from shoes to accessories is available – and all at prices that won't dent your wallet (too much). *3940 Fourth Ave, Hillcrest, T: 619 692 3291.*

Raw ❶ 2A

Trendy, upmarket boutique for women's fashion, including slinky designer denim pieces and a small selection of shoes, bags, and Brazilian swimwear. *940 Garnet Ave, Pacific Beach, T: 858 483 9111, www.rawclothing.com*

Vintage accessories at Wear It Again Sam

Wear It Again Sam ❶ 3B

A much-loved classic on San Diego's thriving vintage fashion scene, Wear it Again Sam was founded almost 30 years ago by Kristine Anderson. If you've ever longed to be a Hollywood diva, here is the place for you to pick up some divine silk lingerie, a dazzling and highly glamorous 50s' ballgown or an elegant silk smoking jacket. There's

Thrift Stores

San Diego has an excellent range of vintage fashion stores, but if you are looking for a serious bargain, head for the thrift stores. Run by associations like the Salvation Army or the American Veterans Association, they are often hangar-sized buildings bulging with second-hand clothes at very low prices. They're very popular with students and young hipsters, but you have to be prepared to rummage.

also a beautiful range of beaded bags, costume jewelry, and Spanish-style fringed shawls to provide the finishing touches. *3823 Fifth Ave, Hillcrest, T: 619 299 0185, www.wearitagainsamvintage.com*

Western Hat Works ❷ 3F

This hat shop has been going since 1922, and offers an impressive selection of just about any hat you care to mention. For men or women, you can find anything from stetsons to Panamas. Open seven days a week, they also offer a hat-cleaning service. *868 Fifth Ave, Gaslamp Quarter, T: 619 234 0457.*

Food & Wine

Chuao Chocolatier ❶ 1A

It may be located in a shopping center, but this celebrated shop is southern California's finest artisan boutique dedicated to the art of chocolate. You'll need to take a slow walk around the shopping center's 150 shops to work off the calories after you make a purchase. *4545 La*

Trader Joe's is a popular healthfood store

Jolla Village Dr, La Jolla,
T: 858 546 8858.

In Good Taste ❹ 4B

If you want to put together a luxurious picnic, look no further than this gourmet emporium with its freshly baked bread and huge cheese selection. There's also a range of beautifully presented gift items and chocolates. *1146 Orange Ave, Coronado, T: 619 435 8356.*

Trader Joe's ❶ 2A

There are hundreds of branches of this well-known healthfood store

dotted across the United States, including a handful in San Diego. The peanut butter is justly considered to be America's finest, and you'll also find an outstanding selection of exotic produce and gourmet food items as well as vitamin supplements and health boosters. *1211 Garnet Ave, Pacific Beach, T: 858 483 0224.*

The Wine Bank ❷ 5F

This shop is acknowledged by most to offer the finest selection of vintages in the city. While the selection of wines from France, Italy, and Spain is admirable, it's the Californian bottles that should attract you. It's also worth giving the Mexican wines a try for something truly unique. *363 Fourth Ave, Downtown, T: 619 234 7487, www.sdwinebank.com*

Gifts & Souvenirs

Babette Schwartz ❶ 3B

For the drag queen in all of us, this wacky boutique is packed with

colorful gifts. Items draw heavily from classic pop and white trash culture. Be prepared to choose from religious kitsch, bright Mexican fiesta ware, Bettie Page emblazoned books, and much more. *421 University Ave, Hillcrest, T: 619 220 7048, www.babette.com*

Cathedral ❶ 3B

Gorgeous candles, soaps, lotions, and potions in one of the best-smelling shops you are likely to encounter in San Diego. And these scented indulgences look as good as they smell, which makes everything

Sweet-smelling potions in Cathedral

Beautiful blooms from Flora Style

Gift-wrapped treats at Original Paw Pleasers

twice as desirable. There are pretty gift ideas from a mind-boggling array of candle-holders to unusual vases and tiles. *435 University Ave, Hillcrest, T: 619 296 4046.*

Flora Style ❶ 3B

Michael and Carlos put together some of the most original and creative flower arrangements in the city, and their shop is always a delight to visit. As well as their striking bouquets, you can also pick up some scrumptious holiday chocolates from the finest chocolate makers on the west coast or choose from the range of bold, contemporary vases and other gift items for the home. *3807 Fifth Ave, Hillcrest, T: 619 299 9092, www.florastyle.com*

The Original Paw Pleasers ❶ 3B

For the pet who has everything. This extraordinary bakery is devoted to dogs and cats and offers a range of pet treats from Doggie Donuts to bone-shaped biscuits – all baked freshly every day. If you're looking for a gift that will last longer than the time it takes to gulp, consider a fetching leopard-print coat and matching hat, sure to please even the most demanding pooch. *2525 University Ave, T: 619 293 PAWS, www.pawpleasers.com*

P.B. Home & Garden ❶ 3B

Brightly colored Mexican pottery, plant pots, painting, sculptures, and other folk-art from south of the border. *3795 Fourth Ave, Hillcrest, T: 619 295 4851.*

Markets

Farmers' Markets

Farmers' Markets are held in neighborhoods across San Diego. Ask the tourist office (see p.50) for a comprehensive list.

Kobey's Swap Meet (off map)

San Diego's biggest outdoor flea market. It offers an amazing variety of goods from fresh food through to clothing, electricals and computers, home and garden goods, and even antiques and collectibles. You are sure to find a bargain if you are prepared to scrum. Haggling, of course, is *de rigueur*. Received advice is to go early and to wear comfortable shoes! *Open 7am-3pm Fri-Sun. 3500 Sports Arena Blvd, Sports Arena, T: 619 226 0650, www.kobeyswap.com*

Shopping Malls & Factory Outlets

Fashion Valley Mall ❶ 2B

An enormous outdoor shopping mall boasting more than 200 smart shops and restaurants. You'll find several department stores here, including

Bright and cheery architecture at Horton Plaza

Taxing Tricks

When you are shopping in the US, remember that sales tax is added at the till. Sales tax varies from state to state, but in California it is 7.25 percent, so always add it to the price marked on the goods you have your eye on. This tax is also added to the final total on restaurant bills.

Macy's, JC Penney, Saks, and Nordstrom, plus lots of other well-known names. *7007 Friars Rd No. 392, Mission Valley, T: 619 688 9113, www.simon.com*

Horton Plaza ❷ 4E

San Diego's best-known shopping center covers a massive seven blocks in the heart of downtown. Its unusual architecture encompasses shops, department stores (including Nordstrom and Macy's), a cinema, and restaurants. *324 Horton Plaza, Downtown, T: 619 239 8180, http://westfield.com/hortonplaza/*

San Ysidro Village ❶ 6C & ❺

Right by the Mexican border, this complex (formerly the San Diego Factory Outlet Center) is adding new good-value outlets by the day. *4498 Camino de la Plaza, San Ysidro, T: 619 690 2999.*

Seaport Village ❷ 5C

A relatively small and touristy mall right on San Diego Bay, with shops, restaurants, street entertainment, and a 19th-century carousel to delight children. *849 West Harbor Dr, Suite D, T: 619 235 4014, www.spvillage.com*

Sports Goods

Dale's Swim Shop ❷ 6A

A tiny boutique offering swimwear to suit all shapes and sizes from

Buy a board at the South Coast Surf Shop

several European and US designers. *1150 Orange Ave, Coronado, T: 619 435 7301.*

The Golf Mart ❶ 4C

An enormous golf supermarket offering a wide selection of famous-name golf clubs, clothing, and accessories and an online shopping facility. *1231 Camino del Rio South, T: 619 298 9571, www.thegolfmart.com*

Pilar's ❶ 2A

Stylish, sophisticated designer bikinis for glamorous women looking to make a statement. *3745 Mission Blvd, Pacific Beach, T: 858 488 3056. www.pilarsbeachwear.com*

Polar Golf ❶ 3B

Choose from an enormous range of accessories. Also offers custom club fitting, rent-out golf equipment, and a shipping service that delivers all over the world. *3877 Pacific Highway, Midtown, T: 619 291 3186, www.polargolf.com*

Beyond the Mall

The car is king in southern California, and the shopping malls have grown up to accommodate this. San Diego is stuffed with malls, but recently the battle against this shopping culture has begun. Independent, quirky shops are mushrooming across the city, acting as little islands of protest against the slick blandness of the modern mall experience. Go beyond the center of town and explore Hillcrest (*see p.8*) and the Gaslamp Quarter (*see p.7*); they are both good neighborhoods for unusual small boutiques and stores.

san diego entertainment

San Diego is the perfect location for a sporting holiday and offers an incredible array of sporting facilities. And whether your idea of a good time is surfing, sailing, golf, or simply lazing on the beach, you are virtually guaranteed fantastic weather. The city also has a strong theatrical tradition: the La Jolla Playhouse was begun by Gregory Peck and other Hollywood stars to give them a chance to tread the boards once in a while and is regarded as one of the best regional theaters in the US. You can check out the latest Hollywood releases at any of the massive cinema complexes found in almost all the major shopping malls, or see cult favorites at a small local cinema. And if you are here between December and March, don't miss the chance to follow a California gray whale on its long trip from Alaska to Mexico.

Cinema

Almost every shopping mall, including the Horton Plaza (see p.24) and Fashion Valley (see p.24), has a cinema complex showing all the latest Hollywood blockbusters.

What's On
The Visitor Center (see p.50) has a helpful free Visitor's Guide to the city with listings of annual events and contact details of the various performance venues, sports stadia, and attractions. It also produces a glossy booklet called *Art and Sol* every six months, which describes forthcoming events, including dance, festivals, film, theater museums, music, and more (available online at *www.sandiegoartandsol.com*). The best listings guide is the *San Diego Reader*, a free magazine available in bars, hotels, and restaurants.

Hillcrest Cinema ❶ 3B
Unusual arthouse and foreign-language films. *3965 Fifth Ave, Hillcrest, T: 619 819 0236.*

IMAX Dome Theater ❶ 4H
San Diego's IMAX theater is in the Reuben H Fleet Science Center (see p.5). Movies are shown on a 76-ft (23-m) domed screen. *Reuben H Fleet Science Center, Balboa Park, T: 619 238 1233.*

Palm trees outside the IMAX in Balboa Park

Ken Cinema ❶ 2B
The Ken is the only cinema in San Diego to still run on a reel-to-reel projector and shows films ranging from foreign-language to remastered black-and-white classics. *4061 Adams Ave, T: 619 819 0236.*

Classical Music & Opera

Classical music performances are often held at city museums, particularly the San Diego Museum of Art in Balboa Park (see p.5). Check the Visitor Center for details.

Balboa Park Organ Recitals ❶ 4F
The Spreckels brothers donated the enormous organ housed in Balboa Park (see pp.4-5) in 1914 provided free concerts were held for the public. These concerts have been going ever since and are now a city institution. *Recitals: every Sunday at 2pm, with additional summer concerts on Monday evenings at 7.30pm in July and August, T: 619 702 8138.*

San Diego Civic Theatre ❷ 3E
The city's major venue for opera, ballet, and theater, including performances by the San Diego Opera, California Ballet, and the La Jolla Chamber Music Society. *1100 Third Ave, Downtown, T: 619 570 1100, www.sdcivic.org*

The Spreckels Organ is housed in Balboa Park

Clubs

Club Montage ❶ 2B

One of the biggest and best-known clubs in San Diego, this flashy club has three floors with state-of-the-art sound and laser systems, and a staggering rooftop bar. It attracts a fashionable mixed crowd.
2028 Hancock St, Middletown,
T: 619 294 9590,
www.clubmontage.com

On Broadway ❷ 3F

Easily San Diego's swishest nightclub, this impressive hotspot is housed in a converted 1925 bank building. Musical choices vary each evening and pump out through a 90,000-watt sound system. Be sure to dress up or you won't get past the velvet ropes. *615 Broadway, Downtown,*
T: 619 231 0011,
www.obec.tv

Onyx Room ❷ 3F

There are two spaces here: a mellow candle-lit cocktail bar at the front, and a fashionable club for

Back room at the Onyx Club

30-somethings at the back. *Open Tue, Thu, Fri & Sat 9pm-2am. 852 Fifth Ave, Gaslamp Quarter, T: 618 235 6699, www.onyxroom.com*

Live Music

The main concert venue is the ipayOne Center (❶2A), T: 619 224 4171, www.ipayonecenter.com. Summer concerts are also held at Humphrey's (❶3A), *2241 Shelter Island Dr, T: 619 220 8497, www.humphreysconcerts.com;*

or the SDSU Open Air Amphitheater (❶2C), *T: 619 594 6947.* For one-off performances and DJ nights, check the flyers at music stores and for smaller concerts, check out the following venues:

The Belly Up Tavern (off map)
While its location in Solana Beach makes it an inconvenient place to go for a bout of live music, this fantastic club is often the first port of call for visiting artists ranging from Ette James to Frank Black. The setting is funky, the music even more so. Tickets often sell out well in advance so be sure to get your hands on tickets before making the 30-minute drive. *143 S. Cedros Ave, Solana Beach, T: 858 481 9022, www.bellyup.com*

The Casbah ❶3B
This battered old local legend showcases new and established alternative and rock bands. *2501 Kettner Blvd, T: 619 232 4355, www.casbahmusic.com*

Big concerts are held at the ipayOne Center

Sign outside Croce's jazz bar

Croce's ❷ 4F

The best known of San Diego's numerous jazz bars, Croce's offers some of the best jazz and blues in two neighboring venues in the Gaslamp Quarter. There's no cover charge if you eat at the restaurant (which is very good) but reservations are essential. *802 Fifth Ave, Gaslamp Quarter, T: 619 232 2891, www.croces.com*

Sevilla ❷ 4E

Restaurant, flamenco club, and nightclub in one, with nightly flamenco guitar performances, as well as dance shows featuring tango, salsa, and flamenco. The club gets going around 10pm and is hugely popular with an up-for-anything party crowd, particularly at weekends. *555 Fourth Ave, Gaslamp Quarter, T: 619 233 5979.*

Theater

Diversionary Theater ❶ 3B

The ground-breaking controversial mixed-gender productions have already led to a number of awards. The small theater is up in University Heights. *4545 Park Blvd, T: 619 220 0097, www.diversionary.org*

Late-night revels at the Sevilla

Recently restored Lamb's Players Theatre

Lamb's Players Theatre ❷ 6A

A year-round program of drama, comedy, and classics in an historic Coronado theater. *1142 Orange Ave, T: 619 437 0600, www.lambsplayers.org*

Old Globe ❶ 4E

It isn't all Shakespeare at this three-

The Globe mimics London's replica theater

theater complex in Balboa Park, but the Bard features heavily on the program, particularly during the summer. The main theatre is an exact copy of the Globe Theatre in London. *1363 Old Globe Way, Balboa Park, T: 619 234 5623, www.theoldglobe.org*

Spectator Sports

American Football

San Diego Chargers ❶ 2B

The chargers play at the Qualcomm Stadium. The season runs from August to December. The Chargers Express Bus (T: 619 685 4900) collects fans from pick-up points around the city for the $10 round-trip. *Qualcomm Stadium: 9449 Friars Rd, Mission Valley. T: 1 877 242 7437, www.chargers.com*

Baseball

San Diego Padres ❷ 5F

San Diego Padres play at PETCO Park. The baseball season runs from April to October and a shuttle bus ferries fans from locations around the city to the stadium for home games. For information, call: *T: 619 795 5000.* For tickets, call: *T: 877 374 2784, www.padres.com*

Golf

San Diego is a golfer's paradise with many and varied courses to suit all standards (*see right*). It hosts one major PGA event: the Buick Invitational held at Torrey Pines (❶1A) in February (for information: Century Club: *T: 619 281 4653, www.buickinvitational.com*).

Del Mar Thoroughbred Racing Club

Horse-Racing

Del Mar Thoroughbred Racing Club (off map ❶ 1A)

The famous Del Mar Thoroughbred Racing Club hosts horse-racing from mid-July until mid-September. For information, contact: *2260 Jimmy Durante Blvd, Del Mar, T: 858 755 1141, www.delmarracing.com*

Participation Sports

Fishing

Fish for free off the municipal piers, or check out companies offering sport fishing. A California fishing license is required for anglers over 16. *City Fish Line: T: 619 465 3474.*

Point Loma ❶ 4A

A wide variety of fishing trips from half-day local tours to 10-day trips down the Mexican coast. *1403 Scott St, Point Loma, T: 619 223 1627, www.pointlomasportfishing.com*

Point Loma is popular for sea fishing

Seaforth Sportfishing ❶2A

This company offers all kinds of packages for all ages and abilities from half-day trips to multi-day or overnight packages. *1717 Quivira Rd, Mission Bay, T: 619 224 3383, www.seaforthlanding.com*

Golf

The Visitor Center (*see p.50*) has a useful Golf Map showing the major

On the green at Torrey Pines

courses, with contact details and information, or try online at *www.golfsd.com*. The following are open to the public and most hire out golf clubs and offer tuition.

Balboa Park Municipal Golf Course ❶4H

A leafy 18-hole course in Balboa Park. *2600 Golf Course Dr, T: 619 239 1660.*

Coronado Municipal Golf Course ❷6A

An 18-hole course overlooking the bay. Make reservations. *2000 Visalia Row, Coronado, T: 619 435 3121.*

Mission Bay Golf Resort ❶2A

An undemanding but scenic course in Mission Bay. *2702 North Mission Bay Dr, T: 858 490 3370.*

Torrey Pines Municipal Golf Course ❶1A

A great municipal course with beautiful ocean views. Reservations are essential. *11480 North Torrey Pines Rd, La Jolla, T: 858 570 1234.*

Horse-Riding

Sandy's Rentals Stable ❶6C

Beach and trail rides on horseback for people of all ages and abilities, located about 15 minutes south of downtown. *2060 Hollister St, Imperial Beach, T: 619 424 3124, www.sandysrentalstable.com*

Jogging

The Embarcadero area in downtown San Diego (❷5C-6D) is a popular spot for joggers, with wide, unclogged pavements and ocean views. There are also jogging trails around Balboa Park, and Mission Bay (❶2A) offers several superb, flat running trails with beautiful views.

Jogging through lovely countryside

Tennis

There are several private tennis clubs in San Diego, but the following are all open to the public.

Balboa Tennis Club ●3B

Twenty-five hard courts, plus 19 lighted courts in Balboa Park. Visitor passes available. *2221 Morley Field Drive, T: 619 295 9278, wwwbalboatennis.com*

La Jolla Tennis Club ●1A

Nine free public courts, including five lighted courts. *7632 Draper Ave, La Jolla, T: 858 454 4434, www.ljtc.org*

The sailing round Mission Bay is superb

Peninsula Tennis Club ●3A

The dozen lighted courts at this private tennis club are available for hire by the public at a very modest fee. *Robb Field, Ocean Beach, T: 619 226 3407.*

Sailing & Watersports

The opportunities for sailing and watersports are almost limitless in San Diego. If you are bringing your own boat, contact the Port of San Diego Harbor Police for information on overnight anchoring, *T: 619 686 6200.* The following rent equipment and/or give lessons:

Coronado Boat Rental ●6B

All kinds of boats on offer here, from yachts to pedal boats. *1715 Strand Way, Coronado, T: 619 437 1514.*

Mission Bay Sports Center ●2A/●3

Rents out sailboats, catamarans, kayaks, and motorboats, and also offers sailing lessons. *1010 Santa Clara Place, Mission Bay, T: 858 488 1004, www.missionbaysportcenter.com*

Spend an afternoon in a kayak

Seaforth Boat Rentals ●2A

Rents out sailboats, powerboats, kayaks, and water-skiing equipment, and runs sailing trips and powerboat cruises. *1641 Quivira Rd, Mission Bay, T: 619 223 1681, www.seaforthboatrental.com*

Windsport ●2A

Rents out kayaks, windsurfs, surfboards, and kiteboards. It also offers instruction, a great selection of kayaking trips, and runs a repair service. *844 West Mission Bay Dr, T: 858 488 4642.*

Biking, Skateboarding, & Rollerblading

San Diego is not ideal for cyclists although some neighborhoods do have cycle lanes. The beaches and the Mission Bay area and Coronado are particularly good places for cycle rides, although the boardwalks can get crowded. The city has several skateboarding parks. The biggest is Bacon St (**1**2A), Ocean Beach, and another in nearby Robb Field (**1**2A), T: 619 525 8486. The smooth, wide paths along the Embarcadero (**2**5C-6D) are popular for rollerbladers, and parts of Balboa Park (*see pp.4-5*) are good to skate.

Bikes & Beyond **1** 5B

Bike and rollerblade rental. *1201 First St, Ferry Landing Market Place, Coronado, T: 619 435 7180.*

Cheap Rentals Mission Beach **1** 2A/**3**

Bikes, surfboards, and rollerblades. *3689 Mission Blvd, Mission Bay, T: 858 488 9070, www.cheap-rentals.com*

Skateboarding in Balboa Park

RADD **1** 2A/**3**

Bike, surf, and skate rental on Mission Beach. *3843 Mission Blvd, T: 858 488 7789, www.missionbeach bikeandsurfrentals.com*

Surfing

Surfing is California's unofficial national sport and the endless beaches in San Diego attract a surfing community year-round. The best surf is at Ocean Beach (**1**3A), Pacific Shore, Mission Beach (**3**), and Imperial Beach (**1** 5B). Further up the coast is beautiful Swami Beach, another favorite with surfers.

La Jolla Surf Systems **4**

Surfboard rental and repairs.

2132 Avenida de la Playa, La Jolla Shores, T: 858 456 2777, www.lajollasurfshop.com

San Diego Surfing Academy

Professional surfing instruction for all ages and levels. *PO Box 866, Cardiff by the Sea, T: 760 230 1474, www.surfsdsa.com*

Swimming

Plunge **1** 2A/**3**

3115 Ocean Front Walk, Mission Beach, T: 858 228 9300.

Downtown YMCA **2** 3D

500 West Broadway, T: 619 232 7451.

And great surfing too ...

San Diego's seafront glowing in the late evening sunlight

san diego places to eat

San Diego has never been as famous for its food as other Californian cities like Los Angeles and San Francisco, but the city's culinary scene is going through something of a renaissance. Top chefs at some of the city's smartest restaurants are winning accolades for their adventurous cuisine, and chic new eateries are springing up almost daily. There is an amazing variety of cuisines on offer, from smart French restaurants in exclusive suburbs to the buzzing bistros of the trendy Gaslamp Quarter. While you are here, don't miss the chance to sample some traditional Mexican cooking, particularly in the Mexican border town of Tijuana. Finish the night with a frozen Margarita in a hip rooftop bar, or nurse a beer within sound of the waves in the surfer neighborhoods of Ocean Beach or Pacific Beach.

taste it places to eat and drink

Price per person
Prices based on a three-course meal without alcohol.
$ cheap (under $20)
$$ inexpensive ($20-30)
$$$ moderate ($30-40)
$$$$ expensive ($40 +)

American

Barbarella $$ ❶1A
Right on the shore in La Jolla, this popular bistro is always buzzing – best to get there early or late if you don't want a long wait. The food is simple, but always fresh and very tasty: choose from pizzas, salads, and soups. *2171 Avenida de la Playa, La Jolla, T: 858 454 7373.*

Corvette Diner $ ❶3B
Step back into the 1950s at this classic diner with leatherette booths, neon signs, loud rock 'n' roll, and crazy waitresses decked out in 50s-style gear. It's a big favorite with kids and teenagers celebrating birthdays, and the burgers, sandwiches, and

Dine next to a vintage car at Corvette

shakes are always good. *3946 Fifth Ave, Hillcrest, T: 619 542 1476, www.corvettediner.signonsandiego.com*

Dakota Grill & Spirits $$ ❷3F
A raucous favorite in the lively Gaslamp Quarter (*see p.7*), offering mouth-watering delights such as pizzas baked in wood-fired ovens, and beer brewed in the attached micro-brewery. *901 Fifth Ave, Gaslamp Quarter, T: 619 234 5554.*

Fifth & Hawthorn $$$ ❶3B
This unmarked eatery in the heart of Hillcrest is a popular place for a network of dedicated regulars. The dark and atmospheric spot features a menu that hasn't changed in decades. Everything is basic but well prepared. Solid staples such as linguine in clam sauce or filet mignon make up the bulk of the offerings. *515 Hawthorn, Hillcrest, T: 619 544 0940.*

The Green Flash $$ ❶ 2A

This popular beach café is a popular hangout for the hip and happening, drawn to the varied menu of American and seafood favorites. Go heavy with a well-cooked steak or fried fish of the day, or choose from one of the ample salads for something a little healthier (yet just as filling). Sunsets from the patio are very popular, so be sure to snag a table well in advance if you want to enjoy the show. *701 Thomas Ave, Pacific Beach, T: 858 270 7715, http://greenflashrestaurant.com*

Hodad's $ ❶ 3A

Surfer-themed burger restaurant with a fun atmosphere, great décor (sit in a surfer van while you tuck into your burger), laid-back staff, and great burgers – they've been voted the best in San Diego for three years running. *5010 Newport Ave, Ocean Beach, T 619 224 4623.*

Perry's Café $ ❶ 2B

This is a big, old-fashioned diner just off the highway, with a long dining counter and friendly waitresses who

Tipping

In California, as in the rest of the United States, a tip of around 15-20 percent for service is considered normal in restaurants. In bars, it's usual to tip around $1 per drink if you are having a cocktail, or a little less for a beer.

have been here since forever. The breakfasts are good and filling, and the house specialty is the range of frittatas – thick, freshly made omelets stuffed with all kinds of filling. *4610 Pacific Highway, Old Town, T: 619 291 7121.*

Asian

Roppongi $$$$ ❹

If you can't make your mind up, Roppongi has the answer: a vast range of tapas-style dishes for sharing, which range from Indonesian shrimp to Mongolian *quesadilla*. There's plenty more inventive Asian fusion cuisine on the main menu (if you've still got room), and you can dine out on the delightful patio or inside in a bamboo-edged booth. It's popular with a noisy, fashionable crowd, and there's a good weekend brunch menu that goes down a treat too. *875 Prospect St, La Jolla, T: 858 551 5252, www.roppongiusa.com*

Royal Thai Cuisine $$ ❷ 5F & ❹

This smart Thai restaurant combines elegant décor, smooth service, and good cuisine at reasonable prices. It's a winning formula that has led to several awards. The kitchen will make

Hodad's – the best burger bar in town

your dish as hot as you want, and there are vegetarian options.
Branches: 467 Fifth Ave, Gaslamp Quarter, T: 619 230 8424; 737 Pearl St, La Jolla, T: 858 551 8424.

Spice & Rice Thai Kitchen $–$$ (off map)

Great Thai cooking away from the crowds. As the place is situated in a business district, it tends to be quiet in the evenings – and becomes all

Beautiful views over the sea at George's at the Cove

Smoke-Free Zones

Since 1998, it has been illegal to light up in California's bars or restaurants. Some bars turn a blind eye to smokers, but it's becoming increasingly rare.

the more romantic as a result. Classic items such as pad Thai and satay are uniformly excellent. *7734 Girard Ave, La Jolla, T: 858 456 0466.*

Californian

George's at the Cove $$$$ ❹

Probably the most popular restaurant in San Diego, offering wonderful cuisine with the accent on seafood, views of La Jolla's famous cove, and impeccable, attentive service. Upstairs you'll find the George's Ocean Terrace and Café ($$), a moderately priced alternative, which has the same views and service but offers a more relaxed atmosphere. Book a table well in advance. *1250 Prospect St, La Jolla, T: 858 454 4244.*

Kemo Sabe $$$ ❶ 3B

It's no surprise that Kemo Sabe is always coming top in popularity polls. It offers some of the most creative Pacific Rim cuisine in town, served up in polished designer surroundings. *3958 Fifth Ave, Hillcrest, T: 619 220 6802.*

Nine-Ten $$$ (off map)

Feel daring? Then head to this restaurant specialising in Californian cuisine and order the inventive 'Mercy of the Chef' set menu. The five-course meal costing $55 (or $80 with wine) changes daily depending on what's fresh at the market in the day. Make sure to leave room for dessert. The peanut-butter pie is delicious. *910 Prospect Street, La Jolla, T: 858 964 5400.*

French & Mediterranean

Bertrand at Mister A's $$ ❶3B

Back in the 60s and 70s, Bertrand's was the place you wanted to be taken to on special occasions. With its stellar views, manicured cocktail waitresses, and crushed velvet interiors in deep red, it was the height of class. A $1 million renovation in 2000 has kept the restaurant on top. The food is average, but the atmosphere and vistas more than make up for this. *2550 Fifth Ave, Hillcrest, T: 619 239 1377, www.bertrandatmisteras.com*

Thee Bungalow $$$$ ❶3A

Easily the most romantic and upmarket restaurant in the surfer paradise of Ocean Beach (*see p.9*), Thee Bungalow is set in a charming little cottage. The classic French and Mediterranean cuisine is accompanied by a well-chosen wine list, and if you get there early enough, you can take advantage of their reasonably priced 'early bird' treats between 5.00pm and 7.00pm. The house specialty is roast duck, served with a choice of delicious sauces. *4996 West Point Loma Blvd, Ocean Beach, T: 619 224 2884, www.theebungalow.com*

Eat at romantic Chez Loma

Chez Loma $$$$ ❶6C

One of the prettiest and most romantic restaurants in town, Chez Loma is set in a 19th-century cottage just around the corner from the Hotel Del Coronado. Dine by candlelight on exquisite French classics in the traditional dining room, or out on the flower-filled terrace. *1132 Loma Ave, Coronado, T: 619 435 0661, www.chezloma.com*

Chive $$$ ❷4E

Hip, minimalist French restaurant in the perennially popular Gaslamp

Quarter that offers sleek, creative cuisine to go with the equally sleek clientele. *558 Fourth Ave, Gaslamp Quarter, T: 619 232 4483, www.sdurbankitchen.com*

The Marine Room $$$$ ❹

The exhilarating ocean views are unbeatable at this beautiful restaurant, universally acknowledged as one of San Diego's finest. The excellent cuisine may be French in origin, but chef Bernard Guillas deftly combines international influences to create some of the most inventive cuisine in California. *2000 Spindrift Dr, La Jolla, T: 858 459 7222, www.marineroom.com*

Mille Fleurs $$$$ (off map)

Mille Fleurs is set in the exclusive neighborhood of Rancho Santa Fe, where celebrities buy their holiday mansions. Probably the most celebrated restaurant in San Diego, it offers contemporary French cuisine and flawless, if formal, service. It's a way from the center of town, but worth it. *Country Squire Courtyard, 6009 Paseo Delicias, Rancho*

Santa Fe, T: 858 756 3085, www.millefleurs.com

Napa Valley Grille $$$$ ❷4E

Downtown workers in-the-know flock to this Mediterranean eatery on the top floor of the Horton Plaza shopping center. Avoid the crowds by going at dinnertime when the appealing dining room serves up delicious grilled seafood, fresh salads and authentic pasta dishes. A great

Stunning ocean views from The Marine Room

rest-stop if you're spending a day shopping in the city. *Horton Plaza Shopping Center, Downtown, T: 619 238 5440.*

Tapenade $$$ ❶1A

This elegant, modern restaurant in the heart of La Jolla has won several awards. It serves fresh Mediterranean and Provençal cuisine and has an excellent wine selection stacked up impressively behind the bar. Black-

Slick chic in the dining room of Tapenade

and-white photographs of Paris set the scene. *7612 Fay Ave, La Jolla, T: 858 551 7500, www.tapenaderestaurant.com*

Mexican

Casa Guadalajara $$$ ❶ 2B

It may be a 'theme' restaurant, but this place is a great option for those traveling with kids. Strolling Mexican musicians provide constant entertainment, portions are huge and the outdoor courtyard is a nice touch on warm days. It may be touristy, but you can't knock the combination of old California atmosphere with tasty Mexican meals. *4105 Taylor St, Old Town, T: 619 295 5111, www.casaguadalajara.com*

El Agave $$$ ❶ 3B

This is slightly off the beaten track, but an excellent modern restaurant offering inventive variations on Mexican staples, and you can also choose from more than 300 tequilas at the bar. *2304 San Diego Ave, T: 619 220 0692, www.elagave.com*

Fins $ ❶ 1A

There are several Mexican chain restaurants in San Diego, but this

San Diego Specialties
Right on the Mexican border, it's inevitable that Mexican food should feature heavily in San Diego. Tuck into the famous fish tacos (*tacos de pescado*), chunks of freshly fried fish in a crispy taco shell, or some spicy *tamales*, corn husks with all kinds of fillings from beef to pumpkin. California's ethnic diversity is reflected in the popularity of fusion cuisine, found at some of the city's fanciest restaurants, which combine all kinds of surprising ingredients from around the world.

one is generally regarded as the best if you are looking for fish tacos, a local specialty. The bright, pared-down décor doesn't encourage you to linger, but it's just the spot for a fresh, cheap snack. *La Jolla Village Square, 8657 Villa La Jolla Drive, La Jolla, T: 858 270 3467.*

Barrels of fun at Zócalo

Pokéz $ ❷ 3G

There are delicious, filling Mexican breakfasts at colorful little Pokéz, and it's always crowded with San Diego's arty youth who appreciate the low prices and relaxed atmosphere. Food is predominantly vegetarian. *947 E St, Downtown, T: 619 702 7160, www.pokezsd.com*

Zócalo $$ ❶ 3B

A laid-back, casual brasserie in Old Town (*see p.10*), serving good burritos and other Mexican favorites, along with a selection of seafood and steaks. *2444 San Diego Ave, T: 619 298 9840, www.brigantine.com/zocalo*

Seafood

Anthony's Fish Grotto on the Bay & Star of the Sea $–$$$$ ❷ 2B

A San Diego staple. There are several branches around town, but this one has the prettiest location overlooking the ocean. There are several restaurants here; if you are looking for a quick, tasty snack, head for the raucous main dining room; for something more formal, there's the adjoining lounge area, where you can sink into a leather chair and admire the views. The Star of the Sea

Anthony's Fish Grotto on North Harbor Drive

restaurant is the classiest experience, with award-winning seafood served in a stylish dining room overlooking the bay. *1360 North Harbor Dr, Downtown, T: 619 232 7408, www.gofishanthonys.com*

Coronado Boat House $$$ ❶ 4B

This charming Victorian wooden boathouse provided the architectural inspiration for the Hotel Del Coronado (*see p.57*). Tasty, fresh seafood and beautiful views across the marina. *1701 Strand Way, Coronado, T: 619 435 0155, www.coronado-boathouse.com*

Vegetarian

Jyoti Bihanga $–$$ ❶ 2B

Perhaps surprisingly in health-conscious California, there are few strictly vegetarian restaurants in town. There are lots of vegan options and occasional Sunday brunch-time feasts (call for opening hours). *3351 Adams Ave, Normal Heights, T: 619 282 4116, www.jyotibihanga.com*

Cafés

Bread & Cie $ ❶ 3B

Light and lofty bakery and café with a staggering selection of gourmet bread, sandwiches, and cakes. Try the fabulous *panella dell'uva* bread (only available at weekends) as part of the breakfast special (a range of breads served with handmade preserves), or tuck into some freshly baked scones and muffins with mugs of speciality coffee. *350 University Ave, Hillcrest, T: 619 683 9322.*

Michele Coulon ❶ 1A

These cakes are truly heavenly – dense chocolate truffle cakes, melt-in-the-mouth lemon tarts with a lacy topping of caramelized sugar – and they are made with only the highest-quality ingredients. The pretty café also serves delicious French cuisine at lunchtime and is open for dinner at the weekends. One visit is not enough. *7556 Fay Ave, Suite D, La Jolla, T: 858 456 5098, www.dessertier.com*

Wondrous, mouth-watering cakes at Michele Coulon

Bars

The Beach at Hotel W ❷ 2D

San Diego's swankiest bar at the city's swankiest hotel (see p.57). It's called 'the beach' because they have brought the beach to the hotel rooftop, and you can sip your cocktail and sink your toes into the heated sand floor. *Hotel W, 421 West B St, Downtown, T: 619 231 8220, www.starwoodhotels.com*

Cannibal Bar ❶ 2A

Remember the Polynesian-themed bars of days gone by? Relive the mai tai madness at this South Seas-inspired bar that offers killer cocktails and live music. It's probably the only place in town where you can still hear slide guitar music on a regular basis. *3999 Mission Blvd, Pacific Beach, T: 858 539 6850, www.catamaranresort.com*

Red Circle Café ❷ 3D

Vast stylish bar, restaurant, and martini lounge in the heart of the Gaslamp Quarter. The martinis are the best in town and there's a seemingly endless variety. Regular DJ sessions. *420 E St, Gaslamp Quarter, T: 619 234 9211, www.redcirclecafe.com*

san diego practical information

Friendly San Diego does everything it can to make visitors welcome and ensure a hassle-free stay. The tourist office is well equipped, and the staff are extremely helpful. There's a wealth of useful information on their easy-to-navigate website, too. The city is typical of southern California, with a series of distinct neighborhoods linked by highways, and a car is the easiest way to get to most of the sights. If you are using public transport, make a trip to the Transit Store in downtown San Diego for the useful bus and tram maps. One of the best ways to see the city is by taking a Trolley Tour, which makes a 30-mile (48-km) circuit of all the main attractions with commentary by the entertaining drivers.

By Shuttle

Many hotels provide a free shuttle service from the airport to the hotel. Other services are available from both terminals to destinations all over the county, with fares starting at $8 for downtown.

Cloud 9 Shuttle Service

T: 858 505 4900,
www.cloud9shuttle.com

Coronado Livery

T: 619 435 6310.

Public Transport

San Diego sprawls across a vast area and the major sights are linked by a complex system of highways so public transport is time-consuming. The one exception to this is the Blue trolley line (*see right*) which is easy to use and links most major sights. Ask at the Visitor Center (*see p.50*) or Transit Store (❷3E), *102 Broadway, T: 619 234 1060*, for timetables and route maps. There are special passes for the over-60s, disabled visitors, and long-term visitors: check with the Transit Store for details.
Information: www.sdcommute.com, T: 619 238 0100.

By Trolley

There are two trolley (tram) lines: the Blue line and the Orange line. The Blue line links Old Town with downtown and runs to the Mexican border at San Ysidro (❶6C/❺). Trolleys run 5am-12 midnight.

By Bus

There are more than a hundred bus lines. Stops are clearly marked with a small blue and white symbol. The Transit Store (*see above*) has timetables and tickets for most routes. Buy tickets on the bus with exact change. Express buses make few stops, so don't get caught out.

Taxis

There are several taxi firms in San Diego. They have different-colored livery and are easy to spot thanks to a lighted TAXI sign on the roof. You can usually hail them on the street, and there are taxi ranks at most malls and outside the hotels.

Taxi Numbers

Crown City Cabs: T: 619 437 8885.
Orange Cabs: T: 619 291 3333.
Silver Cabs: T: 619 280 5555.
Yellow Cabs: T: 619 234 6161.

Tickets & Fares

Fares on the trolleys and buses depend on the route and distance traveled, but usually cost between $1.25-$2.50 for a one-way ticket. There are self-service ticket machines at all trolley stops, but you need exact change for the buses.

Orange line trolley downtown

Day Tripper Pass

These passes are available for one, two, three, or four days and are valid for unlimited travel during the designated time period on trolleys and buses. They cost $5, $9, $12, and $15, and are bought at the ticket machines at trolley stops or at the Transit Store (see p.51).

Car & Bike Hire

For the best car-hire deals, check online before your visit. Insurance is not usually included in the package. To drive in Mexico, ensure that your insurance extends over the border.

Brightly colored cabs for hire

Avis
T: 800 331 1212, www.avis.com

National
T: 619 497 6777,
www.nationalcar.com

Eaglerider ❶ 2A
Rent Harley-Davidson bikes for that Easy Rider experience.
3655 Camino del Rio West, Suite B,
T: 619 222 8822.

Driving Conditions

San Diego is a large conurbation with several centers, which means that everyone drives everywhere. The neighborhoods are linked by a network of highways, and a road map is an essential purchase for all visitors. Traffic is heavy during rush hour (8am-10am and 5pm-7pm).

Parking Facilities

All the shopping malls have parking, which is usually free. There are private parking lots everywhere; pay the attendant as you enter. Roadside metered parking is available, but it is difficult to find a space and you will need a handful of quarters.

Banks

Many banks have 'drive-thru' facilities. Thomas Cook has offices in the Horton Plaza shopping mall, T: 800 287 7362 (see p.24), and American Express has offices close by at 258 Broadway, T: 619 744 3770.

Changing Money

Banks in San Diego offer a better deal than the bureaux de change, particularly those at the border.

Opening Times

Banks are open from 10am–5pm on Monday to Thursday, until 6pm on Friday, and until 1pm on Saturday.

ATMs

You'll find plenty of ATMs at the airport, along any shopping street, in the malls, and at all major attractions.

Pedal-powered taxis can be hired all over town

Disabled Access

San Diego's sights, monuments, and public transport are all accessible to disabled travelers. Pick up the leaflet *Access in San Diego* from the Visitor Center (*see p.50*) for information. Buses and trolleys are equipped for wheelchairs, and the Cloud 9 Shuttle

A wheelchair friendly car park

Service (*see p.51*) has wheelchair accessible mini-vans. Avis, Budget, and Hertz provide hand-control rental cars with 24-hours notice. *Information: Accessible San Diego, T: 858 279 0704, www.accessandiego.org*

Emergencies

To call an ambulance, the fire service, or the police: *911.*

24-hour Pharmacies

Many of the big chain pharmacies stay open 24 hours.

Longs Drug Store ❶ 1B
5685 Balboa Ave, T: 619 279 2753.

Rite Aid ❶ 2B
535 Robinson Ave,
T: 619 291 3705.

Internet Access

Most hotels and hostels offer internet access, but there are not many cafés when you are out and about:

Club LAN ❶ 3B
Costs around $3 per hour and has the best selection of computer games in town. *3545 Midway Dr, Suite J, T: 619 224 3387, www.clublan.com*

Cybernet C@fe 2000 ❶ 5C
Internet access for about $6 an hour. Fax, copy service, online games. *424 Broadway, Chula Vista, T: 619 476 7543, www.cybernetcafe2000.com*

David's Coffeehouse ❶ 3B
Roughly $6 per hour. Relaxed coffee house with internet terminals. *3766 Fifth Ave, Hillcrest, T: 619 237 5000.*

ATM outside Wells Fargo bank

Post box and public telephone

Internet Café ❷ 3F
Expensive ($3 for 15 minutes).
A copying service and a small café.
*800 Broadway, Downtown,
T: 619 702 2233.*

Post Offices

Main Post Office ❸ 3F
Downtown, 815 E St, T: 800 275 8777.

It costs $0.84 to send a postcard to
Europe, $0.63 for a postcard to
Canada or Mexico, or $0.24 to send
a postcard within the US. There are
plenty of dark-blue post boxes on
streets throughout the city.

Public Holidays

Some museums and sights are closed
on public holidays and the transport
system runs restricted services. Some
post offices and banks also close.

1st Jan	New Year's Day
3rd Mon Jan	Martin Luther King Jr Day
3rd Mon Feb	President's Day
Mar/Apr	Easter Sunday
last Mon May	Memorial Day
4 Jul	Independence Day
1st Mon Sep	Labor Day
11th Nov	Veterans' Day
4th Thu Nov	Thanksgiving
25th Dec	Christmas Day

Public Telephones

There are public telephones at the
airport, in the malls, and in bars and
restaurants. Phone cards are the
cheapest way to make calls. Local
calls from private phones are free.

Phone cards come in denominations
of $5, $10, and $20, and are found
in convenience stores and
drugstores. Scratch off the silver
panel to reveal a pin number. Some
cards are exclusively for national
calls, so check in advance.

International Codes

**Australia: 61; Canada: 1; New
Zealand: 64; UK: 44.**

The code for central San Diego is
619. For international calls, dial *011*,
the country code, and the number.

Sightseeing

Opening Times
Shopping times vary. Most shops are
open Monday-Saturday 9am-6pm.
Some small shops close Mondays in
winter. Malls open Monday–Saturday
10am–9pm, Sunday 12 noon-9pm.
Many museums close Monday, and
most open 10am–5pm.

Ticket Concessions
Concessions are available on public
transport and at most museums and
monuments for students, pensioners,

and under 16s. Students must show a student card or an ISIC card.

Tours

Contact Tours
Guided tours by bus of San Diego and Mexico, including the big theme parks like SeaWorld (see p.12), Legoland (see p.60), and San Diego Zoo (see p.11). T: 619 477 8687, www.contactours.com

Coronado Touring ❷6A
Ninety-minute walking tours of Coronado (see p.6) by local residents. 1110 Isabella Ave, Coronado, T: 619 435 5993.

Take an Old Town Trolley Tour

Gaslamp Quarter Historical Foundation ❷4E
Two-hour walking tours around the Gaslamp Quarter (see p.7) on Saturday mornings only. 410 Island Ave, T: 619 233 4692, www.gaslampquarter.org

Old Town Trolley Tours
Open-sided trams that make a 30-mile (48 km) circuit of all the major sights of the city, complete with commentary. Get on or off at any stop point. Also the Ghosts and Gravestones tour, a spooky two-hour night-time city tour. T: 619 298 8687.

Get some fresh air on a sea cruise

San Diego Harbor Excursions ❷3B
Brunch and dinner cruises around the Bay, and whale-watching cruises. 1050 North Harbor Drive, T: 619 234 4111, www.sdhe.com

San Diego Scenic Tours
Guided bus tours of San Diego, Tijuana (Tijuana map), and other sights in Mexico. T: 858 273 8687, www.sandiegoscenictours.com

Walkabout International ❶3B
Sponsors dozens of free walking tours led by local volunteers around many neighborhoods. 4639 30th St, T: 619 231 7463, www.walkabout-int.org

directory

For locals as well as newcomers, this San Diego directory has everything you need to get the best out of the city, from annual events to finding the best hotels in all categories to suit your needs. As well as a special feature on keeping the kids happy, there are suggestions for additional places of interest to visit not included in earlier chapters, and you'll find a page of further reading, listings of popular websites and newspapers to keep you in touch with what's happening, and a feature understanding the locals and speaking their lingo.

Places to Stay

San Diego spreads over such a huge area that you must choose the location of your hotel carefully. For the nightlife and shopping, head for Downtown (see p.6); to be close to SeaWorld and other leisure facilities (see p.12), find a hotel in Mission Bay; for the beaches and surfer hang-outs, try Ocean Beach or Pacific Beach (see pp.9, 11); and for peace and quiet, try La Jolla (see p.8) or Coronado (see p.6).

Cool Hotels

Hotel Parisi $$$$$ ❹

🍽 ‖ ‖ 🍸 ⚬ @ 🛎 ❄ Ⓟ

The hotel of choice for visiting celebrities (including Madonna). All

---

Key to Icons

Hotels

🍽	Room Service
‖	Restaurant
🍸	Fully Licensed Bar
🛁	En suite Bathroom

@	Business Centre
🛎	Health Centre
❄	Air Conditioning
Ⓟ	Parking

Museums

🚻	Toilets
♿	Disabled Facilities
☕	Refreshments
🎟	Free Admission
👥	Guided Tours

Price per room

$ budget (under $70)
$$ moderate ($70-120)
$$$ expensive ($120-180)
$$$$ luxury ($180-250)
$$$$$ de-luxe ($250 +)

the rooms have been designed according to the principles of *feng shui* and you can also try yoga or take a wellness treatment at the indulgent spa. *1111 Prospect St, La Jolla, T: 858 454 1511, www.hotelparisi.com*

W San Diego $$$$$ ❷ 2D

A boutique hotel, favorite with supermodels and stars, with all the luxury trimmings, including a spa and rooftop bar (*see p.47*). *421 West B St, T: 619 231 8220, www.starwoodhotels.com*

Classic Hotels

Hotel Del Coronado $$$$$ ❷ 6A

Affectionately known as 'the Del', this vast luxurious Victorian hotel sits right on the beachfront and was famously featured in *Some Like It Hot* with Marilyn Monroe. Note that almost half the rooms are in a modern annexe, which isn't half as atmospheric. *1500 Orange Ave, T: 619 435 6611, www.hoteldel.com*

U.S. Grant Hotel $$$$$ ❷ 3E

Built in 1910, this centrally located hotel has retained its crystal chandeliers, mahogany furnishings, and the gracious air of another age. *326 Broadway, Gaslamp Quarter, T: 619 232 3121, www.usgrant.net*

Business Hotels

Hilton San Diego Gaslamp Quarter $$$ ❷ 5E

Situated across the street from the Convention Center, this hotel is convenient both for business travelers and those wanting to live it up in the historic Gaslamp district. The generous rooms boast all the amenities you would expect from the Hilton chain. For something really special, book yourself into the intimate Enclave wing – sort of a hotel in a hotel for those looking for that bit of extra luxury and a bit more ambience. *401 K St, Gaslamp Quarter, T: 619 231 4040, www.hilton.com*

Manchester Grand Hyatt $$$$$ ❷ 5D

Right next to the Convention Center, this opulent high-rise offers excellent business facilities, including a special area with desks and office supplies. Great bay views (especially from the top-floor restaurant) and all the luxury trimmings. *1 Market Place, Embarcadero, Downtown, T: 619 232 1234, www.hyatt.com*

Family Favorites

Prava $$$ ❷ 3F

A beautiful boutique hotel in the heart of the Gaslamp Quarter, with vast, plush suites equipped with kitchenettes and crisp linen-covered king-sized beds. A restaurant and bar will open soon. *911 Fifth Ave, Gaslamp Quarter, T: 619 233 3300*

Paradise Point Resort $$$$$ ❶ 2A

Next to SeaWorld (*see p.12*), this resort hotel is set amid lagoons and gardens, and amenities include tennis, golf, swimming, croquet, and bike hire. It offers discounts and kids aged under 17 stay free in their parents' room. *1404 Vacation Rd, Mission Bay, T: 1 858 274 4630, www.paradisepoint.com*

Surfer Hangouts

Surfer Motor Lodge $–$$ 2A

🍴 ⛺ ❄ P

An attractive blue and white painted lodge on the beach in buzzy Pacific Beach, where the nightlife and surf attract a young crowd. Ask for a room with sea views. *711 Pacific Beach Dr, Pacific Beach, T: 858 483 7070, www.surfermotorlodge.com*

Ocean Beach International Hostel $ 3A

🍴 🍸 🛒 ❄ P

A fun backpacking hostel with a few double rooms and four-person dorms. A great location on Ocean Beach, meters from the sea. *4961 Newport Ave, T: 619 223 7873, www.californiahostel.com*

Crystal Pier Hotel $$ 2A

⛺ ❄ P

A collection of cosy Cape Cod-style cottages on the old-time Crystal Pier at Pacific Beach. The perfect choice for visitors looking for intimacy, romance, beachside living and a dash of history. Each cottage has a private deck and the boardwalk is just a short walk away. *4500 Ocean Blvd, Pacific Beach, T: 858 483 6983, www.crystalpier.com*

Other Sights

See also *See it, pp.2-15.*

Coronado Museum of History and Art 6A

♿ 🚻

Exhibits on military aviation between the world wars, the building of the Hotel Del Coronado (see p.57), and famous visitors to the peninsula. *Adm. Open 9am-5pm Mon-Fri, 10am-5pm Sat, 11am-4pm Sun, Apr-Oct, daily until 4pm Nov-Mar. 1100 Orange Ave, Coronado, T: 619 435 7242*

Mission Basilica San Diego de Alcala 2C

🚻

First of the 21 missions established along the coast, with a museum and gardens. *Adm. Open daily 9am-4.45pm. Tours by arrangement. 10818 San Diego Mission Rd, T: 619 281 8449, www.missionsandiego.com*

San Diego Aircraft Carrier Museum 4B

🚻

Giant aircraft carrier USS *Midway CV-41* is home to San Diego's marine history museum. It provides virtual reality flights alongside a comprehensive history of the vessel. *937 North Harbor Dr, T: 619 544 9600, www.midway.org*

San Diego Museum of Man 4E

♿ 🚻

Anthropological museum set in a stunning mission-style building, with a changing program of exhibits on topics relating to international cultures. Set in the historic California Tower in Balboa Park (see pp.4-5). *Adm. Open daily 10am-4.30pm. 1350 El Prado, Balboa Park, T: 619 239 2001, www.museumofman.org*

San Diego County Sheriff's Museum ❶ 2B

San Diego's original prison, with live police communications, a jail, and a courtroom. *Free. Open Tue-Sat 10am-4pm. 2384 San Diego Ave, Old Town, T: 619 260 1850, www.sheriffmuseum.org*

Serra Museum ❶ 2B

A handsome and engaging museum set in a whitewashed mansion surrounded by parkland, which is devoted to the history of San Diego during the Native American, Mexican, and Spanish periods. *Adm. Open Fri-Sun 10am-4.30pm. 2727 Presidio Dr, T: 619 297 3258, www.sandiegohistory.org*

Parks & Gardens

See also *See it, pp.2-15*.

Mission Trails Regional Park ❶ 1C

Extensive national park (5,800 acres) with wild, rugged hiking and biking trails, a golf course, fishing, and a visitor's center. *1 Father Junipero Serra Trail, T: 619 668 3281, www.mtrp.org*

Pacific Rim Park ❶ 3A

A small park designed by students from San Diego's sister cities around the world. *1401 Shelter Island, T: 760 436 3525.*

Quail Botanical Gardens (off map)

Pretty botanical gardens with walking trails and a host of unusual plants, located an hour's drive north of San Diego. *230 Quail Gardens Drive, Encinitas, T: 760 436 3036, www.qbgardens.com*

Kids' Venues

It is hard to imagine a better city for children than San Diego. If the beaches aren't enough, there are dozens of theme parks, the excellent San Diego Zoo (see p.11) and SeaWorld (see p.12), loads of nature parks for hiking and playing (see left), child-orientated museums, and excellent programs of children's events at many other museums.

Kids love all the sports facilities, from skateboarding (see p.35) to surfing (see p.35), and the whale-watching trips (see p.55). The free monthly newspaper *San Diego Family Press* has listings of forthcoming events for children. In addition, try the following:

Giant Dipper Roller Coaster ❶ 2A/❸

A vintage wooden roller coaster and carousel. *3190 Mission Blvd, Mission Bay, T: 858 488 1549, www.giantdipper.com*

Legoland (off map at ❶ 1A)

A vast attraction 45 minutes' drive north of San Diego and especially popular with the under 10s. *1 Lego Dr, Carlsbad, T: 760 918 5346, www.legolandca.com*

Model Railroad Museum ❶ 4G
Railways, trains, and interactive exhibits (see p.5). Casa del Balboa, 1649 El Prado, T: 619 696 0199, www.sdmodelroadadm.com

Reuben H Fleet Science Center ❶ 4H
Simulator rides and interactive exhibits, an IMAX cinema, and a planetarium. 1875 El Prado, T: 619 238 1233, www.rhfleet.org

Annual Events

If you're particularly keen to see something, always check dates with the tourist office. There is a calendar of events at www.sandiego.org and details of forthcoming cultural events at www.sandiegoartandsol.com

Mid-December–mid-March
The annual migration of whales along the California coast (see p.55). A number of special events.

Mid-January
Nations of San Diego International Dance Festival:
www.sandiegodance.org

Late January
Local Marathon:
www.sdmarathon.com

Mid-February
Buick Invitational Golf Tournament: Torrey Pines golf course (see p.33).

Early March
Mardi Gras: In the Gaslamp Quarter (see p.7). Parades and special events.

March 15
St Patrick's Day Parade.

Early April
San Diego Crew Classic: Classic rowing competitions.

Early May
Fiesta Cinco De Mayo: Mexico's national holiday is celebrated with dance, parades, food events, and historical re-enactments.

June–September
San Diego Symphony Summer Pops Series: Concerts under the stars every Friday and Saturday at 7pm on Navy Pier in downtown San Diego.

July 4th
Patriotic parades and fireworks to mark Independence Day.

Mid-July–mid-September
Racing season at the Del Mar Fairgrounds (see p.32).

End July
Gay Pride Parade: In Hillcrest (see p.8) and Balboa Park (see pp.4-5).

August
Summerfest: Chamber music concert series held in La Jolla (see p.8).

End August
World Body Surfing Championship: Held at Oceanside Pier.

Early September
La Jolla Rough Water Swim: Takes place in La Jolla Cove (see p.8).

Mid-September
Thunderboat Regatta: Speedboat racing, concerts, and fireworks in Mission Bay (see p.12).

Late September
Cabrillo Festival: Events to mark the landing on the West Coast by

Spanish explorer Juan Rodriguez Cabrillo on 28 September 1542.

October

Fleet Week: A parade of ships, including the historic *Star of India*, plus surface ship tours and the MCAS Miramar Air Show.

October-May

The San Diego Symphony Orchestra season at the Symphony Hall in downtown San Diego.

December

Port of San Diego Bay Parade of Lights: A stunning display of more than 100 boats lit for the holidays.

Daily Papers

The local daily is the *San Diego Union-Tribune*.

The *Los Angeles Times* and *New York Times* are both easily available.

European newspapers can be found at the bigger hotels and at newsstands in downtown San Diego.

Further Reading

Baby Whale Rescue: The True Story of J.J. **Caroline Arnold and Richard Hewett**. A charming true-life story for four- to eight-year-olds.

Birds of San Diego, **Chris Fisher and Herb Clarke**. A good illustrated guide to San Diego's birdlife.

Historic Rambles Through San Diego, **William Carroll**. Walks through San Diego by a prolific local author who has written several books covering all aspects of the city.

Stranger Than Fiction: Vignettes of San Diego's History, **Richard W Crawford**. Essays on San Diego's colorful historical characters.

Kids' Guidebooks

Around San Diego with Kids (Fodor, June 2003).

More Adventures with Kids in San Diego (Sunbelt 2001).

The Lobster Kids' Guide to Exploring San Diego (Lobster Press 2002).

Websites

www.sandiego.org
The official site of the San Diego Visitors and Convention Bureau. An excellent resource for visitors.

www.sannet.gov
The official City of San Diego website, geared toward the residents but with some good entertainment listings for tourists.

www.sandiegohistory.org
The Historical Society's website offers a fascinating introduction to San Diego's history.

www.signonsandiego.com
The *San Diego Union-Tribune's* (*see left*) website has excellent listings and reviews of bars, restaurants, attractions, and the city's entertainment venues.

www.sandiegohotels.com
One of several websites with comprehensive accommodation listings throughout the city.

speak it

Although English is the mother-tongue of San Diego, most visitors spend at least a day exploring Tijuana in Mexico, where everybody speaks Spanish. Here are a few pointers to help you on your way.

Useful phrases

Hello – **hola**
Goodbye – **adiós**
Goodnight – **buenas noches**
Yes/no – **sí/no**
Please – **por favor**
Thank you – **gracias**
How are you? – **cómo está usted?**
I'm fine – **muy bien, gracias**
Do you speak English? – **habla inglés?**
I don't understand – **no comprendo**
Today – **hoy**
Tomorrow – **mañana**
Yesterday – **ayer**
How much is it? – **cuánto questa esto?**
Where is? – **dónde está?**

When? – **cuándo?**
Left – **izquierda**
Right – **derecha**
Straight on – **todo recto**

At the restaurant

Bill – **la cuenta**
Breakfast – **el desayuno**
Lunch – **la comida**
Dinner – **la cena**
Menu – **la carta**
Starters – **los entremeses**
Main course – **el primer plato**
Coffee – **el café**
Tea – **el té**
Mineral water – **el agua minerale**
Still/sparkling – **sin gas/com gas**
Rice – **el arroz**
Bread – **el pan**
Salt – **la sal**
Pepper – **la pimienta**
Milk – **la leche**
Butter – **la mantequilla**
Soup – **la sopa**
Fish – **el pescado**

Chicken – **el pollo**
Beef – **la ternera**
Dessert – **el postre**
Cheese – **el queso**
Beer – **la cerveza**
White wine – **el vino blanco**
Red wine – **el vino tinto**

Surfer speak

San Diego's thriving surfers' community also has its own language.

Killing it – Doing well on a very big wave.
Farming it – Being pushed off your board by big wave.
Chillin', illin', lampin' – hanging out.
Tube ride – when surfer tucks into a wave briefly and is spat out.
Insane – totally cool (for wave, babe, session...) very high praise.
Eating donuts – really big wipe out.
What's uppers? – what's going on?

A

Aerospace Museum 4
Airport 50
Annual events 60-61
Antique shops 18
Automotive Museum 5

B

Balboa Park 4-5
Banks 52
Bars 47
Bookstores 19
Buses 51

C

Cafés 46-47
Car & bike hire 52
Children's Museum of
  San Diego 59
Cinema 28
Classical music 28
Clubs 29
Coronado 6
Coronado Museum of
  History & Art 58

D

Daily papers 61
Dance 31
Disabled access 53
Downtown 6

E

Emergencies 53

F

Fashion shops 20

G

Gaslamp Quarter 7

Giant Dipper Roller
  Coaster 59
Gift shops 22-23

H

Hillcrest 8
Hotels 56-58

I

Internet cafés 53

J

Japanese Friendship
  Garden 5

K

Kids' guidebooks 61
Kids' venues 59

L

La Jolla 8
Legoland 59

M

Markets 23
Mexico 13
Mission Basilica San Diego
  de Alcala 58
Mission Bay 12
Mission Beach 11
Mission Trails Regional
  Park 59
Museum of Photographic
  Arts 5
Music 30

N

Natural History Museum
  5, 58

O

Ocean Beach 9
Old Town 10

P

Pacific Beach 11
Pacific Rim Park 59
Parking 52
Parks & gardens 59
Point Loma 11
Post offices 54
Public holidays 54
Public telephones 54
Public transport 51

Q

Quail Botanical
  Gardens 59

R

Reading matter 61
Restaurants 40-46
Reuben H Fleet Science
  Center 5, 59

S

San Diego Aircraft Carrier
  Museum 58
San Diego Animal
  Park 11
San Diego Model Railroad
  Museum 5, 59
San Diego Museum of
  Art 5
San Diego Museum of
  Man 58
San Diego Sheriff's
  Museum 58
San Diego Zoo 11
SeaWorld 12
Serra Museum 59
Shopping malls 24-25
Sightseeing 54
Sports 32-35

Sports goods 25
Surfing 35, 58

T

Tax, shopping 24
Taxis 51
Theater 31
Thrift stores 21
Tijuana 13, 63
Timken Museum of
  Art 5
Torrey Pines State
  Reserve 8
Tourist information 50
Tours 55
Transport tickets 51-52
Trolley lines 51

V

Vegetarian restaurants 46
Visitor Center 30, 50

W

Whale watching 55
Whaley House 10
Websites 61

Licensed to AA Publishing by Compass Maps Ltd.

Written by Mary-Ann Gallagher.

Updated by Ryan Levitt

Revision management by Cambridge Publishing Management Ltd.

Pictures © Compass Maps Ltd, Susannah Sayler, Alamy/Ron Niebrugge (p.17), inmagine/Glow Images (p.3), inmagine/Creatas (p.27), inmagine/Corbis (p.14-15) except p.11 & p.12 San Diego Zoo; p.30 iPayone Center & The Onyx Room; p.44 The Marine Room. Cover Images: Richard Cummins/SuperStock, SuperStock

Whilst every effort has been made to trace the photography copyright holders, we apologise for any omissions. We would be pleased to insert appropriate credits in any future editions.

info@popoutmaps.com
www.popout-travel.com
© 2007 Compass Maps Ltd.

Patents Pending Worldwide. popout™cityguide as well as individual integrated components including popout™map and associated products are the subject of Patents Pending Worldwide

AA 3395

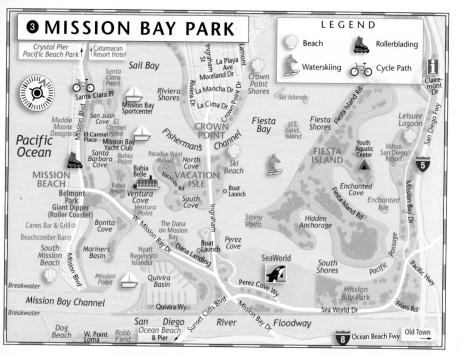

❸ MISSION BAY PARK

LEGEND

🐚 Beach   🛼 Rollerblading

🎿 Waterskiing   🚲 Cycle Path

ℹ️

Crystal Pier
Pacific Beach Park
Catamaran Resort Hotel

Sail Bay

Santa Clara Point

Santa Clara Pl

Riviera Shores

Mission Bay Sportcenter

Maddie Moons Designs

San Juan Cove El Carmel Point

El Carmel Place

Santa Barbara Cove

Mission Bay Yacht Club

Bahia Point

Paradise Point Resort

Bahia Belle

Bahia Resort

Ingraham St

La Playa Ave

Moorland Dr

Lamont

La Mancha Dr

La Cima Dr

Riviera Dr

Crown Point Shores

Crown Point Channel

CROWN POINT

Fisherman's Channel

Ski Islands

Fiesta Bay

U.S. Govt. Island

Fiesta Shores

Fiesta Island Rd

Leisure Lagoon

San Diego Fwy

FIESTA ISLAND

Youth Aquatic Center

Hilton San Diego Resort

Clairemont Dr

Pacific Ocean

Mission Blvd

North Cove

VACATION ISLE

Vacation Rd

Ski Beach

Boat Launch

South Cove

Enchanted Cove

Fiesta Island Rd

Enchanted Isle

Mission Bay Dr

MISSION BEACH

Belmont Park
Giant Dipper
(Roller Coaster)

Canes Bar & Grill

Beachcomber Bar

Ventura Cove

Ventura Point

W. Mission Bay Dr

Bonita Cove

The Dana on Mission Bay

Hyatt Regency Islandia

Boat Launch

Dana Landing

Ingraham St

Stony Point

Perez Cove

Hidden Anchorage

South Shores

Pacific Passage

Pacific Hwy

South Mission Beach

Mission Blvd

Mariners Basin

Mission Point

Quivira Basin

SeaWorld

Perez Cove Wy

Mission Bay Park

Breakwater

Mission Bay Channel

Breakwater

Quivira Wy

Sunset Cliffs Blvd

Mission Bay Dr

Sea World Dr

Friars Rd

Dog Beach

W. Point Loma

Robb Field

San Diego Ocean Beach & Pier

River

Floodway

8 Ocean Beach Fwy

Old Town

know it practical information

Tourist Info

International Visitor Information Center ❹ 4E

*11 Horton Plaza, First Ave & F St,
T: 619 236 1212, www.sandiego.org*

La Jolla Visitor Information Center ❹

*7966 Herschel Ave, Suite A, La Jolla,
T: 858 456 1700,
www.lajollabythesea.com*

Downtown Information Center ❷ 3E

Free tours of downtown San Diego,
highlighting efforts at revitalizing
the neighborhood. *225 Broadway,
T: 619 235 2222,
www.sandiegodowntown.org*

Special Tourist Passes

San Diego Passport

The San Diego Passport costs $79
and is offered by Old Town Trolley
City Tours (*see p.55*). It includes
admission to San Diego Zoo (*see
p.11*), San Diego Museum of Art (*see
p.5*), and the San Diego Maritime

The offices of Old Town Trolley Tours

Museum (*see p.7*); a harbor tour;
a discount shopping booklet from
Horton Plaza (*see p.24*), a phone
card, and a shopping card for
Seaport Village (*see p.25*). Buy at the
Visitor Center or Old Town Trolley
Tour offices, *T: 619 298 8687.*

San Diego Airport

San Diego's airport (❶ 3B) is 3 miles
(5 km) north of downtown. There
are three terminals: 1, 2, and the
Commuter Terminal, which is used
for the shuttle from Los Angeles.
Terminals 1 and 2 have information
booths, ATMs, and cafés. All are
linked by a free shuttle bus service.
*Information: T: 619 400 2400,
www.san.org*

Terminal 1 at San Diego airport

Getting into Town

By Bus

City bus 992 runs between the three
terminals and downtown. The one-
way fare is $2.25 and exact change
is requested. The journey time is
roughly 15 minutes.

By Taxi

There are taxi ranks outside
Terminals 1 and 2. Count on paying
around $10 plus tip (10-15 percent)
for a trip to downtown San Diego.